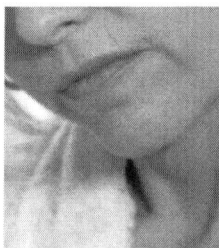

A Change of Plans

Letting go of our plans & watching God's unfold.

Kerri Kilcoyne

Change of Plans

A Change of Plans
Published by JK Ministries
26861 Christy Dr.
Chesterfield, MI 48051

ISBN-13: 978-0692365472
ISBN-10: 0692365478

Special "Thanks" to Todd Oswald for Cover Design & Art Work – "You're Awesome!"

I dedicate this book...

To my mom, who made it all look so easy. To my children, who watched me fail over & over again and yet still made me feel like I was the best mom out there. Lastly, to my husband, who has supported & cheered on every crazy plan I have ever had.

Thank you!

Dear Mrs. Bentley ~
Thank you for loving Jesus in front of me during my childhood. It's women like you who helped me become who I am today, and I'm forever grateful!
Kerri R. W. copy
Psalm 116:1-2

TABLE OF CONTENTS

__Forward__

"Train up a child in the way he should go,
Even when he is old he will not depart from it."
Proverbs 22:6

Sounds good doesn't it? Of course that verse
assumes a parent actually knows the "way he
should go." As Kerri points out in **"Change of
Plans"** she didn't. Or should I say, WE didn't. We
thought we did. But a "Change of Plans" was
necessary to raise the type of children God
wanted us to raise and become the individuals
He could use to minister to others.   With 13
years of pastoring, counseling, teaching and
writing marriage, parenting and family
curriculum, "Pastor" Kerri has a unique
understanding of what real problems a parent
has with their children...... "The apple doesn't
fall far from the tree." With brutal honesty, Kerri
tells of her journey to change from the "fairytale"
she created, to the reality God wanted, which we
can now say is the way it was truly meant to be!

   – Joe Kilcoyne

<u>INTRODUCTION</u>

I think many times, as women, we go into "life" with a plan. When the plan doesn't pan out we are left with some of the hardest decisions we will ever have to make. 1.) We can allow God to make our mess into something beautiful or 2.) We can fight to keep our dream alive.

I really believe, looking back, that God took all of the decisions completely out of my hands. That may sound silly.... but I knew what I had wanted, I just didn't know how to get there. Where I was headed would never have brought me here! Somewhere along this journey, I believe God plucked me up off the road I was on and placed me on an entirely different route. Initially, I was so angry. When my temper tantrums didn't convince God to put me back, I fell into a deep pit of depression. It was in the pit that God began to do a work in my heart. It was in the darkness, that God healed me and restored me.

I've come to realize that most women aren't living "their dream". Somewhere between there and where they are, disappointment grabbed hold of their heart. They have gone from big plans to merely survival. 3 babies in 35 months, newly married, planting a church and parenting a teenager was not my idea of a fulfilled life. I was exhausted and surviving was all I COULD do. What happened to the romance, lavish lifestyle, the "nights out on the town" and expensive vacations? WHAT HAPPENED TO THE HAPPILY EVER AFTER?

Often God permits "chaos" to get us where we need to be. If I hadn't gone through the valley, I never would have learned to fully trust God. My relationship with Him would be one of tradition and religion. Instead, there's an intimacy He and I share. Through every storm, He has shown Himself strong and steadfast. He has spoken to me and carried me when I couldn't handle another moment. I wouldn't trade those days for anything!!

My prayer is that by reading the pages in this book, you'll have the courage to dream again. That this time around, you will allow God to map out the course for your life. It may not look like you want it to, immediately. However, when He is finished, I'm certain you will find that it's exactly the way you wanted it. No, it won't be the fairy tale you've dreamed about since girl-hood. There is no Prince Charming or romantic Balls to attend. But wrapped up in the middle, you'll find that you've fallen more in love than you've ever dreamed possible. You'll see there's more adventure and more romance in being a mom than Cinderella any day. And at the end of your journey, you will find that things couldn't be any better than it was.... If God is allowed to direct your paths.

So read on, my dear friend....and together, we will climb up out of the pit we are in and start again. Gods got big plans for your life. You just have to learn to get out of His way and let Him be God!

> – Kerri Kilcoyne

Chapter 1

It's not what you think...

Philippians 3:10

"That I may know Him and the power of His resurrection and the fellowship of His sufferings, being conformed to His death."

There is a difference in knowing about God and knowing God intimately. Most Christians know about God. They know how the earth was created, how the story ends and all the amazing stories in between.   That's a great place to start but there are very few who know who God is; intimately and personally. As a Christian mom, I have come to the conclusion that the reason few people know God is because parents are raising their children on lessons and stories rather than on experiences and encounters based on the Bible.

We live in such a fast paced world; a sort of microwave society where we have lost sight of the "Be Still" moments in our homes and with our children. We are not experiencing the power and grace of Almighty God on a daily basis but, instead, telling ancient stories and hoping that our children get an understanding that we don't even have ourselves.

Don't get me wrong, those ancient stories are the stories that have shaped and molded my life. In fact, if it weren't for those stories of so many God- fearing men and women; I don't know where I would be today. The problem is that we often end with those stories. We read and read and we study the scriptures, sometimes day in and day out. We attend bible classes and Sunday schools so we can learn more about those stories.

Until we make those stories personal – they amount to nothing. They do us and our families no good. They are just that: stories! God never intended for you to "just know" stories of what He did in days past. It wasn't His plan for you to make it a practice of "reading stories". No, He intended much more. He wants to continue to show Himself strong to His people, even today. It takes more than just knowing stories in order for that to happen. It's a daily living and walking out your faith so that He can prove Himself over and over again...just as He did thousands of years ago.

My prayer is that through this book a fire will be lit deep on the inside of you; a fire that drives you to know the God of Abraham, Isaac and Jacob. My prayer is that you no longer are satisfied with "just" the stories of the bible but that you crave your own stories with the Creator of the Universe. It's those stories that will leave a lasting impression on your children. It's the moments when God shows up in your home or in your workplace or when He exposes Himself to your family that your children will be convinced that there really is a God. It's then that they will begin their own journey of knowing, intimately, the God of their parents.

That really should be our goal as Christian parents. I wouldn't be satisfied if my children ONLY knew about Daniel and the Lion's Den or Jonah and the Whale. Of course, those things are vital to the foundation of every believer but I long to go deeper with them. I want them to see that God still delivers and heals. I want them to see that He is still just as mighty and powerful as He was in the days of Samson and David; that He can be as real and as personal as He was with Mary while she stood at the foot of the cross. This can only happen if I live out my faith in front of them in a very real way. This can only occur when after the stories are told they see them walked out in person. It's not enough to simply tell them that God can heal – if they never see Him heal, that truth will never be passed on.

I have read countless parenting books with all sorts of techniques and tools to help me become a better mom. If it's by a Christian author, I have read it. I never realized that I had been living out a parenting book of my own, written by the greatest Author out there: God! I never went out looking to write a book. I just know that the situations God has brought me through have changed my life and my prayer is that it will change yours.

This isn't your typical parenting book! It really has nothing to do with your children. It's more about you as their parent, your heart, your plan and your relationship with God!

"More is caught than is taught" with our kids. This doesn't give us permission to not have a plan but it does put strong emphasis on "truth". John 8:32 says "And you shall know the truth, and the truth shall make you free." It's your job to find out what "truth" is and then live it to the best of your ability in front of your kids. When they see that what you teach is what you live, their lives will be forever changed!

Chapter 2

What's Your Plan?

Jeremiah 29:11-13
11. For I know the plans that I have for you,' declares the Lord, plans for welfare and not for calamity to give you a future and a hope.
12. Then you will call upon Me and come and pray to Me, and I will listen to you.
13. And you will seek Me and find Me when you search for Me with all your heart.

Change of Plans

The only thing I ever wanted to do, when I grew up, was be a wife and a mother. I wanted to be married and I started looking for my husband around the age of 12. I, now, have a 15, 14 & 12 year old of my own and watching them makes me laugh out loud at some of my own wild schemes and planning.

As I grew into my teen years, I never really liked babies and yet I longed for the day that I would have one or two of my own. Like many little girls, I liked to play "house" and in my fantasy world my children were beautiful and well behaved and my handsome husband adored me. It was very similar to all of the "Disney Princess" sagas except this one was real, at least to me!

After graduation, I started college and dropped out after 2 years due to many distractions – mainly boys! One in particular had taken my eye and seemed like good marriage material; he was cute. That was it! He had no desire to be married and I knew it but I had hoped that I could change his mind. I would play wife, typing his papers and ironing his collared shirts for his class the next morning, while he was out on the town, doing who knows what? Obviously, I got tired of that and moved on.

When I came home, I finally met the man that I would marry and I couldn't have been more thrilled. He loved the Lord and I knew in my heart of hearts that he was the man that God had planned for me all along. He was different. I couldn't put my finger on it but I felt things for him that I had never felt before; including the reality of this elaborate "dream". We dated about 8 months and were engaged. 10 months later, we were married.

The dream finally was a reality and let me tell you – it looked NOTHING like the dreams of my youth. He was a "man's man" and very independent. He did his own thing while I ran around trying to play June Cleaver; baking, cleaning, cooking in dresses and pearls yearning for his attention and yet he rarely noticed. We were both young and immature and were trying to "play" marriage. We were failing miserably.

A couple of weeks into "the dream", I found out that this marriage thing was really my worst nightmare. It wasn't "make-believe" and I couldn't dictate the fairy tale ending. The romance I had envisioned was more like a battle-field and I learned real quick that dreams are just fantasy and there isn't really a happily ever after. Well, not for me, anyway.

As a newlywed, I discovered that the television romances never really show the "ever after"? I'm certain a little girl's ideals and dreams would dramatically change if she found out that marriage took work and parenting was the hardest job she would ever encounter. That her Prince Charming would wake up with messy hair and bad breath and her babies would be disobedient and whiny. I remember feeling slightly angry with Disney after my wedding day. They were always about "the pursuit" and "the conquest" and rarely did they show the lives of these couples after they obtained their prize. All of a sudden I had to figure out how to live with someone who had far different dreams than I. Imagine that? My husband had his own dreams? This was never part of my plan.

The Pastor who married us didn't give us a book and so we had to figure this one out all on our own. In my fantasy world, we knew how to live with one another peacefully, there were no fights and everything was great happened just as I had planned.

Five months after we said "I do", I was pregnant. Again, not part of my plan but with just a little glimmer of hope, I got excited for the dream that could be. Maybe it was this baby that would bring the real joy I desperately wanted. My husband, now father, would turn magically into my Prince Charming, waiting on me hand and foot all the while my beautiful baby girl would sleep soundly through the night and never cry. What a horrible shock that was!

From day one, God began to do a work in me that only He could do. Life wasn't all about me. In fact for the first 8 years of marriage, it was nothing about me. Three children born in 35 months left little time for this mama. I learned very quickly that my needs and desires needed to put on a back burner or should I say they were put there for me. My first born little girl needed a real mother with passionate visions in order for her to grow into that God breathed woman I desperately wanted her to be. I wanted to be that mom for her and for the children that came after. I just had no idea how to get there.

I didn't realize until Abigayle was about 10 years old that God had been busy creating in me the person He desired. He was changing and birthing in me His dreams and His visions for her life and mine. Those truly were some of the hardest years of my life. It was as if, everything I had wanted and the plans that I had made had all been stripped away so that, ultimately, He could replace them with His.

From the time I was very young, I felt such a strong desire to be used by God even though I was trying so desperately to create a magical life for myself. I had no idea that in order for God to use me, to the fullest, it would take me dying. Not dying in the physical sense (although it often felt like that) but my plans and pursuits had to die. I couldn't have any plans if I wanted to fulfill His.

I have always been a dreamer and I dream BIG. If I were to attempt to put some of my dreams on paper people would think I was crazy. What amazes me, even today, is that God's dreams have always been bigger than mine. Until I line my dreams up with His – none of them will come to pass.

Most Christians say they want what God wants. I have learned that what they really mean is they want what God wants as long as it lines up with what they want. It isn't until we lay down our wills and pick up His that He begins to do amazing things that only He can do.

Jeremiah 29:11 says "God knows the plans He has for us. They are good plans and not evil ones. They are plans that will give us an amazing future and a hope." One continual theme that has run throughout my life-time is that my plans usually aren't His.

I can't go "full speed ahead" and expect God to chase me around making it good. It has never worked that way and God isn't going to start now. For years, Jeremiah 29:11 has been my favorite life verse. I quoted it and it excited me to think that I was going to be "somebody" someday. So I lived my life waiting for God to do the impossible and use me for His glory.

A few years into my adult life I read on from verse 11. It just so happens that verse 12 and 13 says "if I seek Him with all of my heart I would find Him." It's in the "finding" we fulfill God's plan for each of our lives. That's the heart of parenting. I have to seek Him to find Him. I have to find out what His plan is and what He wants to accomplish in this role of mother and wife. I have to find out what His plan looks like. It may not look like me, in fact, it probably won't look at all like my plan but I know and can trust that it is good.

Change of Plans

I am so good at running ahead of God because I think I have it all figured out. I have had to force myself to "seek Him" every day for my children and for myself. "What do you want me to do today, God? What do you want me to put into my children and how do you want me to do it?"

When I do that consistently He overwhelms me with great success. Before I can reach the heart of my children, I have to reach God's. If I don't, I may end up with little bits of success and little bits of accomplishment but neither they nor I will ever fulfill God's ultimate plan for our lives.

I want all of God. I want all of what He wants for me, for my husband and for our family. I want my children to have the heart of God. I want them to love Him with all their heart, soul and mind. I want them to trust Him and know Him intimately. None of this can be accomplished in my own strength and according to my dreams. The greatest parenting program out there will not accomplish God's plan for my children's lives. My plans and programs will only complicate and confuse things. I have to seek Him daily. I have to spend time with God and find out what He wants me to do. When I do, He lays out for me the best parenting plan around.

Chapter 3

Becoming Their Editor

Psalms 139:13-16

13. For you formed my inward parts; you knitted me together in my mother's womb.

14. I praise you, for I am fearfully and wonderfully made. Wonderful are your works; my soul knows it very well.

15. My frame was not hidden from you, when I was being made in secret, intricately woven in the depths of the earth.

16. Your eyes saw my unformed substance; in your book were written, every one of them, the days that were formed for me, when as yet there was none of them.

Psalms 139 has been a favorite of mine for years. There is such peace knowing that God had plans for me and for my life before I was even born. What has intrigued me, about the this portion of Psalm 139, is this "book" (*vs 16 Your eyes saw my unformed substance; in your **BOOK** were written, every one of them, the days that were formed for me, when as yet there was none of them.*) that was written for each one of us by God, Himself. In fact, He says that every day of our life was recorded before we have ever lived one of them.

It's my belief that God has recorded in this book all the days He has planned for us. However, there is no guarantee we will live out His plans for our lives. (...and He also knows that). Sometimes, we write our own book and desire God to chase us around, blessing us regardless and then throw fits when He doesn't. No wonder the world wants little to do with God. It's us, Christians, who have consistently given Him a black eye!

Jeremiah 29:11 says that our days will be filled with adventure and blessing. It's here that God tells us He has a great future for each one of us. He doesn't stop there! He tells us how to obtain those promises and that by seeking Him with all of our hearts we would find Him. It sounds so simple and still too many Christians live from failure to defeat and back again. They suffer hardship and financial calamity. Their relationships are a mess and their health is deteriorating. This isn't the plan God had written for us; not according to Jeremiah! It's in the seeking that we begin to find that out.

In fact, the bible says the devil comes for one purpose only – to steal, kill and destroy but Jesus came to give us abundant life (*John 10:10.*) It sounds to me like the devils goal is to rewrite every chapter in your book with failure and depression. He wants your pages to be filled with misery and doubt and they often are. Somehow, we more accurately live out the devils book and blame God for our failed story line. Instead of realizing that God never intended for your life to turn out the way it has. We have just chosen to follow the writings of the enemy rather than the once profound and fulfilling book that was originally penned by Almighty God.

Becoming a parent brings on a whole new perspective as we begin to see ourselves as the editor of this BIG book God has already written for our children. As parents, our goal is to make sure that our kids live out the lives God has planned for them. You can be a purposeful editor and train them up in the way they should go or by default you will edit their book haphazardly and their life becomes more of a crap shoot. Unfortunately, more times than not the latter usually takes place in the parent/child relationship. We parent what we know and what we have been taught.

The majority of parents don't understand their job or the responsibility that comes with being an "editor". As their children grow into adulthood they wonder what went wrong and often blame peers or society for their way-ward kids. When you begin to see yourself as the editor of the book God wrote for your kids, parenting becomes more of an essential necessity and everything else gets put on the shelf until mastered.

A good editor of a good book has to understand the heart and intent of the original author. In fact, world renowned authors will pay good money to get the very best editors. Authors understand that the look and story line in their book can change if their editor doesn't do their job correctly.   They want people who know what it takes to be an editor.

Good editors understand the vision and the objective of the original author. They have the same vision and they realize "creative liberties" isn't an option. They really are dead to their own self and their own dreams. Simply put, they look for flow, grammatical errors and misspelled words and they fix it.

As my first daughter turned 6 months old, I began to feel the overwhelming sense of responsibility for her life. I was a little taken back by the thought that God would trust me with the future of this beautiful little girl. I never was really good at babysitting and couldn't be trusted with anything of any value, as a child myself. Just out of high school, I held a nanny position for two little boys and even lost one of them. I wasn't good at this "kid-thing" and having one of my own was more than I could handle. When she was around 4 months old, I tried telling her the gospel story of Jesus because I wanted to make sure she accepted Him as her Savior and I knew it was my job to teach her the scriptures. Every day became more and more intense.

It all came to a head one October evening. It had been an incredibly difficult day and I was feeling more overwhelmed than usual. As I sat on my bed trying to have my daily devotions with the Lord (out of habit not out of relationship), I slowly began to put into words everything that was going on in my heart; all of my fears and frustrations and how I didn't think I was up for the job-as if He didn't know.

This was very difficult for me to admit because for the last 6 months, I wanted everyone to think I knew what I was doing. For the first time in a long time, I began to hear God speak to my heart. He asked me one simple question: "Are you willing to place Abigayle on Abraham's altar of sacrifice?"

I had been raised in the church, I knew the story. Abraham had been promised a son and after Sarah had given birth, Abraham was asked, by God, to sacrifice him on an altar. Abraham rose quickly in the morning and took his son and did what no man could fathom. Just as he began to worship God with his sacrifice (Isaac), God sent a ram to take his place. There was great rejoicing in Abraham's obedience and Isaac lived.

It was an amazing story of trust and devotion. I knew the right answer to God's question was "of course"! As soon as I uttered those 2 small words – the conviction and the tears fell! I knew I was nowhere near placing that precious little baby on any altar for any sacrifice. In fact, if I was real honest, it was quite the opposite. I didn't trust anyone with her,

including God. There was so much fear that
something would happen that in order to have
any peace, I would literally have to see her at all
times. She slept in our room right next to my
bed. I would have my mother come by to watch
her so I could take a shower. When my mom was
unavailable I would bring her car seat in the
bathroom and sit it right next to the shower and
I would leave the curtain open.   I was in so much
fear that the thought of placing her on an altar
completely paralyzed me. Why would a gracious
God bless me with such a sweet baby only to ask
for her back?

The simple answer is; He knew that if I was
to going to be the editor of the "Abigayle book",
He and I needed to be on the same page. He
needed to remain the Author and I needed to
take my rightful place as the mere editor; no
vision, no objective and no story line.   I had to
give her back to Him. She wasn't mine to keep.
If she wasn't handed over willingly, my
insecurities and fears would inevitably fill her
pages. Her story would change.

That night, I had an all-important decision to make and I did just that. In the midst of my tears, I began the process of obeying my Heavenly Father in what seemed to be the hardest thing I have ever had to do; trusting God in regards to giving him final authority in her life and mine.

Unfortunately, it all wasn't over in that moment. I regularly have to place her, along with my other two, on that altar. Some days, I have to do it every hour. Especially now as they are in their teen years, I feel like it is done by the moment. I want the heart of their author to fill every page of their great big amazing book. That can only happen when I get out of the way. When I recognize that my children belong to God for His use and when I allow Him to do with them as He pleases, He goes overboard with blessing and favor.

Some days, it is the hardest thing in the world for me to trust God with my kids. Actually seeing that statement on paper looks ridiculous. Who better to entrust them to than the One who created the Heavens and the Earth; the One who created them?

This world is crazy and every day they face more and more injustice. Often, my mind gets the best of me and by the end of the evening I am exhausted with worry. Some days, I try and try to give my kids back and I still fail.   I rejoice in the fact that God knows my heart is on a continual journey just like Abraham. The day will come when I will pass the test just as he did and God will send a ram in the thicket to take the place of any harm that may have come to my children as a result of me holding on a little too tight.

That should be the goal for every parent. I am certain you will agree, it isn't easy. Probably more accurate; it's the hardest decision you will ever have to make. The truth is, if you don't make that decision, the book that was written for them, by God, gets a different ending.

Eventually our children become their own editors. They will have to learn how to get out of the way and align themselves with the heart of the great Author. How much easier it will be for them if they were raised with that idea from birth. God is so wise. That is why He said in Proverbs 22:6 "train up a child in the way they should go and in the end they will not depart." He knows that the regularly sacrifice of life is vital to the full completion of His book. Our goal, as parents, is to teach them to become incredible editors; to pay attention to the details and purposes of God and to make sure that their books look exactly as He wrote it.

Chapter 4

Jehovah Rapha
(The Lord who Heals You)

Exodus 15:25-26

25. Then Moses cried out to the Lord, and the Lord showed him a piece of wood. He threw it into the water, and the water became fit to drink. There the Lord issued a ruling and instruction for them and put them to the test.

*26. He said, "If you listen carefully to the Lord your God and do what is right in his eyes, if you pay attention to his commands and keep all his decrees, I will not bring on you any of the diseases I brought on the Egyptians, for I am **Jehovah Rapha**, the Lord who heals you."*

Change of Plans

Five months after my first daughter was born, I found out I was pregnant again. To make matters worse, we had been living with my folks, trying to save money to buy our first home when it happened.

Talk about a very embarrassing moment; having to tell my mom and dad that they would be having another grand-baby. Of course, they were thrilled AFTER my dad asked..."in my house?" He has always had a way of "driving it home" with us kids.

I wouldn't tell anyone I was pregnant with this baby for fear they would start comparing us to rabbits. Besides, I couldn't even form the words in my mouth for the first three months without crying. I was just getting used to relying on God with Abigayle. Two babies was an entirely different story. To top it off, I had gained 60 lbs. with the first pregnancy and you don't lose all 60 lbs. in five months. I had struggled with eating disorders and was underweight before I had gotten married; So 60 lbs. made me plump but not obese. It appeared as though

God was beginning to break that vicious disease by allowing another pregnancy where I eventually gained an additional 60. When God does a work in your life, He never does it the way you think He should.

Looking back, I can see that a bit of depression set in during that pregnancy. My dream of the perfect life was starting to really fade and I felt like everything in my little world was spiraling out of control. I was like a puppet while someone else made all of the decisions for me.   Things were just "happening" and I couldn't do anything about it.

This pregnancy was different than my first. I didn't enjoy it! Actually I hated being pregnant. I was so uncomfortable and it had little to do with the pregnancy. The whole idea of two kids simply overwhelmed me. I knew that amount of stress on a baby in the womb couldn't be good and yet there was nothing I could do to shake it.

By the seventh month mark, I started to have some complications. My doctor put me on

bed rest for the remainder of the pregnancy.
Let's be real for a moment: How exactly does
one care for a baby who started "running" at 10
months, while being on bed rest? It helped that
we were still at my parents' home but this wasn't
at all a part of my plan. Any joy that I had left
had been completely eradicated.

Baby #2 arrives 5 weeks too early and
weighs in at 5 lbs 6 oz. She has so many health
issues and had to spend ten extra days in the
NICU. On July 4th, 2000, while she is still in the
hospital I came face to face with Jehovah Rapha
(my healer). It was early in the afternoon and my
dear husband was taking Abby (our first born)
for a walk around the block in her stroller. The
hospital calls and my heart sinks.

Apparently, my brand new baby, sweet
Alexis Renee', had stopped breathing for an
unknown reason and they were rushing her
down to do a spinal tap to find out what went
wrong. The doctors wanted us there immediately
to sign waivers. My mother flew from her
kitchen table, jumped in her car and sped off to

get Abby and her daddy. For the next 5 minutes
I was completely alone; angry at a God who
would allow something like this to happen.

I stood to my feet in an attempt to get my
shoes on and crumbled. In the middle of my
parents living room I cried out to God like I have
never in my lifetime. It wasn't just because of
the "current crisis" but everything that I had felt
for the past 2 years. With every bit of passion
and strength, I screamed out: "WHERE ARE YOU,
GOD?" And for the first time, in my life, I heard
Him speak in an audible voice.

He said ever so softly, "I have never left!"
That one statement spoke volumes. Somewhere
along this journey, I walked away from Him.
Somewhere, I got discouraged and refused to
trust Him with my life; that maybe He had a plan
and knew what He was doing.

I think we all do that at times. Something
happens that we weren't prepared for and
although we have claimed to trust God, it usually
is conditional. "Ill trust you, God, as long as

nothing unexpected comes my way" or "Ill trust you, God, as long as it all makes sense." When it doesn't, we don't actually say we don't trust Him, but our heart throws a temper tantrum. We worry, we get angry and we get so comfortable with our fears that we don't even recognize we have walked away from the only ONE who can help. We begin to rely on our senses and our past experience or doctors and what they say that it becomes so natural to walk according to what we know (or think we know) rather than by faith.

Parents, listen to me, your children need to see you run to God during your time of crisis. They need to see you walk out your faith. It's not enough to teach them the Word of God. You have to live it every single day at every turn and every trial. Your kids are watching to see if you really believe what you teach or if it's just a story you tell.

That day changed so much for me. I realized how spiritually weak I really was. I knew the bible. I had been raised in the church from birth and I could tell you every story and how it ended. I could even tell you the lesson we should learn from the stories but I never made them personal. I thought because I knew it, I must be living it. What a foolish thought.

This is, truly, the problem with so many of us "so called" Christians. We have been in church long enough and we know the right things to say but if they never become a reality for us our kids will never know the God we were taught. This is usually why we see teenagers walk away from the church and their faith as they grow into adulthood. They haven't been exposed to the "real deal". They feel as though they have been lied to and so desperately want to see truth that they will turn to the first thing that looks real. Their parents are left wondering what went wrong.

Christianity isn't a book or a church. It's a way of life. We can't teach that God heals and yet forget to even ask Him when our kids take a fall. We are so quick to grab the band aids and peroxide (without even thinking) and yet asking God to heal is the last thing on our minds.

In our home, there have been many times, when our children have been rushed to emergency but not before we have prayed. It's amazing what that small step does in the hearts of our kids. Our children know where to turn when crisis hits because we knew where to turn.

It isn't just something we pretend to believe so as to teach our kids to pray. We KNOW that God is the ultimate Healer, the Great Physician. If you don't know that truth deep in your heart you will never be able to teach your kids the true gospel of Jesus Christ.

Prayer or involving God in every area of our lives has impacted our children in ways I never would have imagined. They know where to go for every need or fear or hurt. That can only be taught as you, mom and dads, begin to really walk out your faith and trust in God. It doesn't end with prayer but everything that the Bible teaches us. Your children read the same bible you do. They know what you are supposed to be doing and what you aren't. You can't fool them. When you try to just preach the stories and the moral conduct but don't live it – you can bet that your children won't either.

This parenting book really isn't about your kids at all. It's about you! It's about you building such a strong relationship with the Lord. It's about you relying on Him for answers to some of life's hardest questions.

Chapter 5

For Such A Time As This…

Genesis 2:24
24. Therefore a man shall leave his father and mother and shall become united and cleave to his wife, and they shall become one flesh.

Change of Plans

Since I was a little girl, I wanted to be the "best" at everything. Even though, I never was the "best" at anything. That desire to supersede everyone else's gifts and talents was so strong (ridiculously, strong). In my dream world, I was always winning awards for volleyball or softball. I was the best speller and no one could understand how my 5th grade science fair project was that of an experienced scientist. Reality would say that I could play volleyball about as good as everyone else my age. I could hit a softball 6/10 times and my projects had been done 100x's over.

To say I was the best was a far stretch from the truth. I did go to a national spelling bee once but I didn't come close to winning. I had visions for days of hearing my name announced in front of a crowd of excited parents as the" #1 Speller in the USA". To my dismay, I misspelled a word rather quickly and can't even remember who won that afternoon but I know it wasn't me!

I don't know where that desire to achieve greatness came from. I'm certain a room full of psychologists would have a hay day trying to discover the whys and how's in my life. Never the less, I still see it creep up from time to time; whether it's at a church social with food or a speaking engagement with a bunch of women. I want to be successful! That isn't such a bad thing as long as I am successful according to the standard that is written in the Word of God.

Success, according to God, looks nothing like success, according to the world! It's been quite the journey discovering the vast difference between the two. The moment I get praised for anything I do is the red flag of worldly success. The moment, however, all eyes are drawn to the only true successful One – I know that I have achieved the kind of excellence I was born for.

When it comes to raising my children, it's been no different. I struggle with wanting them to be amazing for God and just wanting them to be amazing. God's been dealing with me on that issue for years and sometimes I get it and other times I fall flat on my face. One thing I have learned is that if my kids are going to bring any glory to God then my standard has to be His standard.

So many Christians live with the "good enough" mentality and they wonder why their kids don't look to the Word or even live a life that's pleasing to God.   He has a very definitive standard that He desires all of His children to live by. As parents it's our duty or obligation to find out what that standard is and then be instructors of that standard for our children. It's not enough to just teach the standard but we as parents must also live by that standard if we genuinely want our children to achieve spiritual greatness.

I have no greater dream for my kids than for them to be used by God and for His glory. The scriptures talk of the disciples shadow healing the sick. That's my dream for my kids. I don't want them to just be good Christian leaders in their little worlds but I want them to do the impossible. We have heard it said that if you want to be something no one has ever been then you need to do something no one has ever done.

Years ago, as I was spending some quality time with my Heavenly Father, He brought me to Genesis 2:24. As I was reading the account of "Creation", this verse jumped off the page at me. I had heard it every time my husband performed a marriage ceremony and every time I had attended a wedding. This day, God was showing me something I had never seen before; "for this reason a man shall leave his mother and father and cling to his wife. "He was showing me that He gave me my 3 children for this exact moment in time; the moment that they would leave our home and our covering and cling to their God-given spouse. The day when everything we taught and instructed would no longer matter because they were now their own people with their own belief system, forming their own families.

Prayerfully, it would resemble a little of what was lived out in our home but there is no guarantee. I'll be honest; the lump that formed in my throat as I read and re-read that verse has never left. It took some time for it all to process but to think that I had a very specific detailed job to do in the next 18-25 years put an extreme amount of pressure on me. These weren't my kids to keep (a resounding theme in my life). They were given to me so that I could teach and train them to be amazing spouses, amazing people and amazing disciples. There is so much to teach. There is so much they need to learn before that day and more than anything I want to do this one right!

So here I was in the middle of trying to do everything right to a place I had never been before. I not only had to teach my children respect and manners and right from wrong so they could be paraded around as amazing kids but they needed to know real life solutions to real life problems they would encounter as adults. The goal now changed from the here and now to the "rest of their life". They needed to know about tithing because tithing is the secret to financial prosperity. They needed to learn about authority because if they didn't stay under the covering of an authority figure they would experience much pain. They needed to learn how to really seek after God because more than anything if they didn't know Him; they wouldn't make it out of this world alive.

It was at that moment that God began to show me the big picture. All along, my dream as a child was to grow up and be a mama and wife. I envisioned cradling sweet babies with bonnets and blankets and dressing up for romantic evenings on the town with my honey. God placed that dream in my heart for more than just the fairytale. He gave me those desires so that I could birth "world changers".

When Jesus was born, I am certain that Mary fell madly in love with Him. What healthy normal mother doesn't? The first time a mother looks into the eyes of her sweet baby or kisses those infant lips she is hooked. It's as if the world stands still for those precious first moments of life. It's in those moments that we envision amazing things for this tiny sweet baby...and then.... the chaos begins.

The draining activity of constantly redirecting and training, teaching and correcting hour after hour creates in us a desire to just make it through each day, alive. I'm confident that Mary knew Jesus was destined for greatness. Her approach to His life and His ministry was vastly different than the majority of most mothers, I assume.

Typically, we just want to survive the day. The moment that we begin to really understand the "greatness" our children were created for changes our entire perspective. The big picture starts to take shape. It's not enough to "just survive", there's too much my children need to know and when fatigue sets in, the "big picture" propels me forward.

I am certain that the day Mary stood at the foot of her son's cross, the thoughts of His childhood ran rampant through her mind. "I wish I had more time. I wish He was still a baby. I wish I could do something to fix this." I am also certain that all of her regrets flashed before her. "I wish I had spent more time hugging and holding, I wish I didn't get so frustrated when He disappeared in the temple, I wish I had prayed more for Him." Mary didn't know that her life with Jesus would end at age 33 and she did the best she knew to do. The bible gives us advance notice that, although, our kids won't be put on the cross there is coming a day when they will no longer be ours. We have to spend our few years with them wisely.

It's not enough to just teach children different techniques and practices. It's way more than that. Our children have to know in their hearts that prayer works and God is real! He is the only lesson that will give our children any success in life. Every day, I am on a quest to show my kids the reality of Jesus Christ. Our family prays together about everything and when we see the answers to our prayers, it's discussed and we rejoice together. I want my kids to know what to do when trouble, sickness or fear comes. That can only be taught when we do these things in front of them and when we see God perform

His Word. More than anything our kids need to "know God and the Power of His resurrection". As long as they have Him, I have nothing to fear.

Chapter 6

Sheer Determination

2 Corinthians 12:9-10
9. But he said to me, "My grace is sufficient for you, for my power is made perfect in weakness." Therefore I will boast all the more gladly about my weaknesses, so that Christ's power may rest on me.
10. That is why, for Christ's sake, I delight in weaknesses, in insults, in hardships, in persecutions, in difficulties. For when I am weak, then I am strong.

Change of Plans

There are 4 basic personality types, according to the historic Greek physician Hippocrates (460-370 BC) that everyone falls into: Phlegmatic, Melancholy, Sanguine and Choleric. It's best to simply define them through a story: There's a house that has caught on fire. The Choleric starts running towards the house with buckets of water, giving orders to anyone who is nearby and able to help. The Melancholy is taking time to create a carefully constructed plan of the best tactics and schemes to distinguish the blazing fire. The Phlegmatic doesn't do anything because he knows someone else will take care of it and the Sanguine shouts, "Let's roast marshmallows!"

My personality has changed multiples times throughout my lifetime usually based on what works and what can get the job done. Sometimes my personality has been formed simply because of the task at hand. There has always been one thread that has weaved itself throughout my entire existence: That of the Sanguine!

Quite honestly, I love to have fun. I can usually find humor in anything even when it isn't appropriate. Unfortunately, some of it has become a sort of "coping" skill that I wish hadn't been developed.

When the ridicule or jokes get pointed at me, I can laugh as hard as the rest. I've always been the one that people enjoy making fun of because "I take it so well." You would be surprised if you heard some of the things Christian people have said to me or about me, all in jest, of course. They laugh, I laugh and everyone thinks all is well; except the real me. I've enjoyed putting on this, sort of; play to make people believe I am strong and capable and able to take on the world.

There's only been one that I have allowed into this private world of mine; my husband. He knows the truth –I often get pushed to the limit and break. I am reminded time and time again that it's in my weakness that He (God) is made strong. I hate that the real me is really a very weary breakable little girl. I'm, often, scared to take the next step and yet somehow trying to convince everyone else that "leaping is my middle name"!

On the other hand my husband usually has the answers and knows exactly what to do. He is the stable one in our relationship. He has no extreme highs and no extreme lows; He is constant and it, honestly, drives me nuts! I have, however, learned to lean on his stability, through the years, to help keep me sane.

I am the passionate dreamer and he is the logical realist. He weighs the pros and cons and I jump before putting on my life jacket. He never spends money foolishly and I never have a penny to my name. He is the brains to our family and I am the heart.

During the first 6 years of marriage I had come to believe I was such a failure, compared to him. My insecurity levels had plummeted to an all-time low and nothing seemed funny anymore. In fact, I started to dislike everything about me and blamed him in the process. I had come to the place where I didn't like who God had created me to be. I wanted to be smart and logical just like him. I wanted to be in control of my emotions and make wise decisions. I hated being wrong not because I was wrong but because I wasn't smart enough to be right.

The devil certainly knows what to whisper when he wants to trip you up. From the time my first child was born he began, discreetly, showing me every bit of in adequacy that I had in my life! Let me tell you, he is good! I went from "let's have fun" to "let's just survive!"

It was about this time that I decided I wanted to Co-Pastor with my husband. You see, everything about my husband was perfect, in this make believe world I tended to live. He could do anything he put his mind to and he always had the answer to every problem. He never failed at anything. I, on the other hand, failed at everything. The day we were leaving with my first child from the hospital, I couldn't even dress her. It infuriated me that he wanted to try. Of course, I wouldn't let him (because I know he could do it) so I called for the nurse and allowed her to put the pretty little "going home" outfit on this tiny little baby.

I had gotten to the place where I decided that if he could pastor a church so could I. It wasn't until years later that I got the picture of God's plan for my life. I, now, know that had I not gotten to that place of complete exasperation, I never would have stepped into my calling. I don't have that kind of guts or stamina and if it wasn't fun there was no point.

One afternoon I, very boldly, told Joe that I wanted to preach. Who was I trying to kid? I couldn't even read a bible verse in a small group, let alone, put a sermon together and publically give it. My sheer determination of proving that I was just as capable as my amazing husband spurred me on.

Surprisingly, he gave me a date and my journey of pushing through intimidation and relying on God's strength began. The big morning came and I was a nervous wreck. I spent the night before in the bathroom and my stomach was a ball of nerves. I panicked and told Joe I couldn't do it. My husband isn't a quitter and he wasn't about to let me quit. He prayed with me and pushed me out of the office into the sanctuary where I would preach my first message. I stood at the pulpit with my knees shaking, hoping I wouldn't vomit all over everyone and I slowly started to speak.

God is so amazingly faithful. It took me stepping out in faith, opening my mouth and once I did, He took over. Joyce Meyer's says, "when God asks you to do something and you are afraid...do it afraid!" That's exactly what I did that day but I didn't end afraid. I believe that day was the start of the "calling" I felt decades before. I slowly started emerging from that very gray time in my life and. For the first time in a long time, felt sparks of excitement for what was to come. I can't remember what I preached. I am certain that if I were to hear it replayed today I would laugh at how ridiculous I sounded. What I do remember is the revelation I got that day of the scripture II Corinthians 9:12-13; God will make me the strongest when I feel my weakest.

As a parent, it's been a journey of learning to trust God. There are days that I have no idea what to do and fear completely paralyzes me. No one learns or grows from my lack of movement. Then there are days that I have no idea what to do and I step out in faith and God takes over. I understand now that most of parenting takes sheer determination. Not just to make it through the day but determination that says, "I'm going to do what God has called me to do, regardless of how I feel,"

From the time my kids were little whenever we would lose something (which was frequent with me); we would take the hands of our little children and ask God to show us where it was.

EVERYTIME we have done that, God has answered. There are people at our church who will come to my kids and ask them to pray for something they have lost because my kids have such a confidence that if we pray, God will answer.

It was a Sunday afternoon and my whole family went to a beach in another city. My father brought with him a brand new bocce ball set. All the grandkids had played with it most of the afternoon and we were finally putting it away for a long drive home. There was one ball missing. We looked and looked and to our dismay couldn't find it. My three kids and I, finally, grabbed hands and asked God to show it to us. We looked a little while longer and decided it wasn't worth the time and decided to leave without it.

As we walked away, my 8 year old (at the time) ever so innocently asked, "Mom, why didn't God show us where the ball was?" My stomach ached. I couldn't leave now. There was no way my kids were ever going to think God didn't answer prayer, not on my watch. So, by myself, with that same sheer determination I had behind the pulpit, I began to talk to God in a way I hadn't before.

"God" I said, "You can't leave it like this. We have trusted you to show us so many things before; if we leave without this silly little ball, there will be 3 children who will forever remember this day as a day you didn't answer. Please God, for the sake of my kids, show me that ball."

You won't believe it but I literally walked right up to it, picked it up and ran it back to my kids. I was so excited to see that, once again, God wanted to prove Himself to my children but wanted me to step out with some sheer determination and trust Him. It was in my weakness that He once again was made strong.

I believe that most of us don't step out in faith in front of our kids because the fear of "it not working" is too great. We worry that God won't look real and our kids will, maybe, doubt. So rather than attempting to believe God, we do nothing.

God has taught me over and over again that He wants to make Himself real to my kids

MORE than I want them to see Him. It's not that He isn't able to do the impossible without a step of faith – He just doesn't.

Over the years and with countless leaps of faith under my belt, I don't know who has been more blessed; my kids or me. Either way, I know that when I decide to do what I am supposed to do even though I am weak, He truly becomes strong! It's those moments that have shaped my parenting. The confidence that it produced in me has helped me reveal exactly who God is. Our kids need to see the reality of God or their relationship with Him will only go so deep. It's our job to find out for ourselves first.

CHAPTER 7

What You Lack
In Skill…

Philippians 4:13
"I can do all things
through Christ who
strengthens me."

Change of Plans

There comes a time in everyone's life when they realize they just aren't good at everything. In fact, for some of us, there comes a time where we realize there is very little that we are good at.

I am a very relational person and, fortunately, my personality has made up for my lack of brains. I can be witty and charming and can enjoy life with the best of them. Yet when it comes to problem solving or history and science I can't compete. I have always felt as though God forgot to give me that part of my brain when He created me and I've struggle with insecurities for years.

It's the same with parenting. I have come to realize that when it comes to children I rarely know what to do. You would think after teaching parenting classes for as many years as I have that I would be able to logically come up with a plan of attack when faced with various struggles throughout my own children's lives.

Change of Plans

If you, on the other hand, were to come to me and ask me for solutions, I could regurgitate everything I know from the books and classes I have taken. It all works but while I am in the midst of crisis in my home – I freeze. It takes me a lot longer to figure out what to do and how to approach a situation than I think it should. I often stumble and react rather than proactively teach and train.

The one thing that I have come to understand, to the fullness, is that If I would simply love my kids and enjoy being with them and they knew it – a multitude of "sins" would be covered. Some of my best "parenting" takes place while we are being silly together.

My son has been playing basketball since he was in kindergarten. I'll be honest when he started, we were a little worried. He wasn't very talented. He was tall for a kindergartner but lacked so much skill. The first practice we wondered, if maybe, we had made a wrong decision. He didn't know what to do with the ball nor did he know how to make a basket. As we gathered our belongings and made our way into the car, we prepared ourselves for a much needed pep talk. He didn't say much as we were driving home and neither did we. We just waited.

After school the next day this little guy went out to our basketball net and began shooting hoops; One after another and then another, At 5:00, Daddy came home and we ate dinner only for him to return outside and continue shooting more baskets. This went on for weeks. This was more than a little boy playing outside. This was a little boy who knew he lacked the skill to be a good basketball player and decided the only way things would change was through hard work and practice

We started noticing this quality in other things. One year we all went to Pennsylvania for a family reunion. Someone brought "hillbilly golf" and he attempted to play. He was horrible and he knew it. Nobody seemed to care as he was only 8 years old and it was just a game. To him, it was more. Once again he started throwing ball after ball trying to get a "ringer"...trying to get good. Even as the majority of the family left to explore the park, he wanted to stay there with an uncle, he barely knew, so he could continue practicing...by himself.... No competition just trying to become good at a game he knew nothing about.

He has done this with so many things; Papers in school where his penmanship was unsightly. Without a word, he would re-write and re-write the same paper asking after each how his writing had improved. Skateboarding was no different and neither was soccer, football or baseball. He was a kid who wasn't happy until he mastered whatever it was he put his hand to.

I have learned so much from this little boy. This child is me. The only difference, I didn't spend near as much time getting better at the things that had me. Feelings of defeat would stop me from even trying. Deep in my heart I knew I would never be as smart as or as talented or as strong as the next. I hated that I had to work so hard at everything and so I often wouldn't.   I was the lazy version of my son.

I have come to the place in my life where I believe with all my heart the verse that says; "I can do all things through Christ who gives me strength". I memorized that verse as a child and often wondered when it would start working for me. When would God show Himself strong in my life and when would I be the "best" at something? Many a nights, I would pray for God to make me smart or make me talented and yet nothing changed.

I have learned that my lack of ability has nothing to do with God. He has always been strong. He has always been smart. He has always lived inside of me. So if the problem isn't Him then it has to be me.

It dawned on me one day that the key to this verse is "I can". I had focused so much on the end of the verse that I lost sight of the fact that it all started with "I". There was something I

was required to do in order for God to do what
He does.

God required movement out of me. He
required practice and perseverance. When I had
done all that I knew to do – He would take it
from there. The Scriptures are chocked full of
verses that deal with "working". The bible even
tells us to "work out our own salvation with fear
and trembling". It says that God will bless the
"work of our hands".

To think I could do nothing and God would
just come in and make me magnificent, makes
me more of a puppet than His child.

Even with my own kids, I would encourage
them to try new things, to step out in faith. If
they got to the end of themselves, almost
defeated, I would rush to their side to help them
accomplish the task at hand. As an earthly
parent I knew that I needed to see some effort
from them before I jumped in.

Change of Plans

I think for so many of us we want to be good at parenting or our job, a hobby or even a ministry. If we weren't born with those skills we think there isn't a possibility of success and we settle; limiting ourselves and God.

But that verse...I can do all things.... That verse changes everything. The Status quo is no longer acceptable. That verse means that I can't be satisfied with my bad attitude or my bad parenting skills. It means that regardless of how I feel, I can get up every morning and spend time with God because I know without Him I am going to fail. When I am exhausted and would love an extra hour in bed but drag myself out is often the mornings of great intimacy with my Heavenly Father.

It means that when my daughters are bickering for the 110th time, this morning, and I don't think I can handle another moment, but force myself to be calm... It's then that God often does a work in their heart that only He can do and the atmosphere in my home changes instantly.

Change of Plans

It means that when my son has ripped another pair of jeans, and I am running low on cash but force myself to remain calm and trust the Lord – it's those days, extra money flows in or bags of hand-me-down's from a friend with children just a little older than mine.

"I can" means that with a little persistence and practice, I can be the best mom for my children. I can train them up in the way they should go. I can do what I was called to do and to the best of my ability and when all of my ability runs out, I can trust that God will expose how truly strong He is. But it ALL starts with "I can".

We are a culture so governed by our emotions. If it feels bad, we cry or lose our cool. If it looks bad, we panic and worry. But God desires more from His children. He desires more especially if we want to see Him show up in our daily lives and in the lives of our kids. He isn't a magic fairy – He is a parent.

Change of Plans

We can't sit around waiting for God to magically change us; to wave His fairy wand and make us a godly mama who trains and instills deep truths into the lives of her kids, regardless of the stress of a situation. He is waiting for us to show Him that we mean business; that we are serious about really becoming doers of the Word. As we begin to seriously walk out our faith – as we begin the "I can" – He will always show up making us stronger and wiser than we really are. It isn't that God isn't willing. He just isn't willing to do it ALL for us.

Chapter 8

Don't Give Up!

Ephesians 6:13b – 14a

"When you have done everything to stand, stand therefore"

Change of Plans

As God slowly removed every bit of my dreams for my life and replaced them with His – my life seemed to take on a new appearance–. Things that were once most important were replaced with things that would last an eternity. I began realizing that I was literally giving every part of my life to other people...and I liked it.   In 2002, my husband and I took on the greatest endeavor of our lives. Again, something not in the plan (the on-going mantra for my life) but something that came together so very flawlessly. We look back now and laugh at how obvious God was in setting us up in our destiny and yet at the time couldn't quite see Him working.

As I sit here and remember those early years I am reminded that Gods ways are not our ways and His thoughts are not our thoughts. I am amazed at how simple it is to follow God's plan for your life and yet how trivial we make it.

There was a large denominational church that had literally disintegrated. At its peak, 500-600 people were being ministered to, weekly. Somewhere along the line, someone got off scripturally and morally and the once booming evangelical church had turned into a ghost town. 14 people were left to pick up the pieces. My husband just so happened to work with one of them. Soon after, he was asked to come and do a bible study with the remnant. One thing led to another and in 2002, Faith Christian Center was born.

Our very dearest friends joined us and really were the reason we even dared to accept the task before us. It was exciting and challenging and we were living the pastor's dream. Everything was coming together so nicely; growing quickly from 14 to 60 almost overnight! 2 years into this amazing journey the same dearest friend stole over $100,000 from the up and coming F.C.C. Everything seemed to stand still. As you can imagine the questions and fears and doubts rose quicker than the morning tide. The thought of having to tell my family that we failed or worse yet explaining to the faithful 60 that it was over was more than this mama could take.

Change of Plans

Funny, now, how all this time later, I look to those years as some of the most precious times of my life. Times when I would cry out to God and I knew He heard me; Moments when I literally felt His presence with me as a daddy comforting a wounded daughter. It was a time when I grew up spiritually, quickly. A time when I had to decide if I really believed everything I said I believed. God, proved Himself over and over again. To be honest, as strange as this is to put on paper, I'm so grateful for those years. It was during those desperate years, I became intimately acquainted with God. Who would have ever thought I would be able to say that?

Well, the church didn't close its doors but it wasn't a success story like you would hope. It was months and years of rebuilding and regaining vision; many tears and many late night prayer meetings trying to get a grasp on what had gone wrong and why?

It wasn't just the money but mortgage payments and utilities that hadn't been paid that really put us into a bind. We had our own bills but decided that we couldn't dare take a salary check from a church that had no money. So for many months we just lived off our own savings until things got better. We had to truly walk by faith and not by sight and I'll be honest, it wasn't as glamourous I would have liked.

Regardless, we did trust God or at least attempted to trust Him. What He did for us during that time of our lives was literally life changing. I now can, confidently, tell people that God cares for them and I believe it. I can tell them that God has a way out of any situation and if they would just attempt to trust Him, He will prove Himself. There is such a confidence that I have in my Heavenly Father that could have only been produced through a crisis. For that, I am eternally grateful.

At the time, we had 3 small babies and a 15 year old foster daughter. My husband would work at the church every day except Wednesdays. Wednesday was my day to do the administrative stuff that needed to be done and he would play "stay-at-home daddy". It wasn't ideal but it worked for us. Wednesday was also a day that I knew nobody was around and I could just pray or worship or talk to God as loud or as quiet as I wanted. There was one Wednesday that I remember feeling as though I wanted to give up. We had eaten enough "church pantry food" to last a life time and my babies just didn't have all the cute baby stuff that every mom desires for their kids.

I was feeling sorry for myself and began to share with God what was going on. As I was crying out to Him, a lady came to the side door and knocked. No one ever came to that particular door and so it surprised me but I opened it to her anyhow. She didn't say much, she just waved a $100 bill in front of my face and said that God told her to give it to me. I was shocked but because we were at the church – I asked her if this was for the church or for me. She quickly said, "Honey, this money is for you – use it however you want." She left; I closed the door and collapsed on the office floor. God cared about this mama's heart. It was at that moment that I realized He really truly loves me and He is willing to do whatever was needed to prove it.

The overwhelming feeling of knowing you're loved by the God of the Universe will give you strength to walk out the toughest of life's journeys. The scripture says "God wants to give you the desires of your heart"! That scripture is true if you allow Him. That $100 got our groceries for the week – real groceries that I picked out. There wasn't a veggie can in my cart. I was elated but God wasn't through. Every Wednesday for the next 3 weeks, that woman came to the side door and handed me another $100.00 bill; no real conversation, no questions asked. The week that our new treasurer and Joe decided we could finally start taking a little bit of a salary check was the last week I ever saw her.

There are countless stories just like this one. It was thru these encounters that God proved His faithfulness. This is just one of many times where God proved His faithfulness to me. He never promised we wouldn't go through the storm but He did promise that He would never leave us. He has been with our family every moment of every day. He has seen the good, the bad and the downright ugly and yet He loves me. He really loves me.

Having that wisdom has paved the path to my parenting. There isn't anything I wouldn't do to transfer that wisdom to my children and yet I know that they will have to learn that lesson on their own. You don't learn lessons when there are no trials. You learn lessons when you are forced to make a choice. My children have seen me cling to the scriptures when everyone else said do something else. They have seen us walk out the Word when we felt like it and when we didn't.

More is caught then is taught – my prayer is that one day when they are forced to choose, the choice will be an easy one. My hearts cry is that one day, they too, will be able to have such a confidence in their Creator that nothing could change their mind; that they will cling to the Word of God in hard times and in good because they know intimately in whom they believe in. I want them to know, deep in their hearts, that God truly loves them. That He thinks about them and cares about the little details of their lives. I want them to have real relationship with the Lord Jesus Christ and I know that they have had to see me do it first. That's really what parenting is all about; living the same thing you teach. Before you can do that you have to know what it is you really believe. We have the ability to raise "world-changers" and it starts with us knowing the one who changed the world.

Whatever you do, weary Mama, DON'T GIVE UP NOW!

Change of Plans